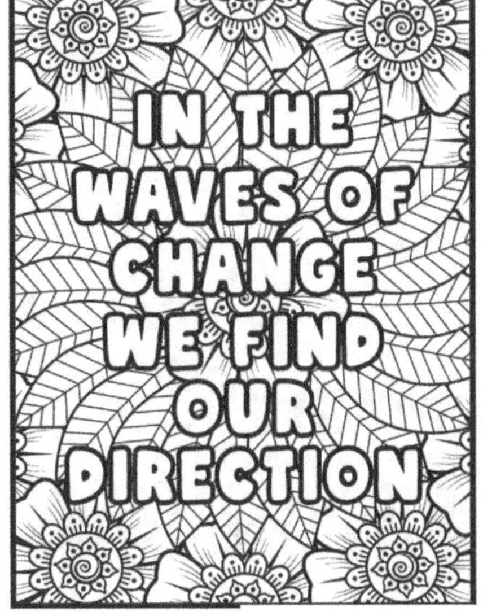

THIS BOOK BELINGS TO

We create our book love and greatcare
you mistakes can always .for any issues
with your Book, such as faulty binding
,printing errors, or something else
please do not hesitate to contact us at :
razib.bera45@gmail.com
we will make sure you get a
replacement copy immediately.
For any suggestions or question
regarding our books, please
Thank you

IF YOUR
DREAMS
DON'T SCARE
YOU
THEY ARE
TOO
SMALL

IN THE
WAVES OF
CHANGE
WE FIND
OUR
DIRECTION

YOU ARE
WHAT
YOU DO
NOT WHAT
YOU SAY
YOU'LL
DO

BE THE
REASON
SOMEONE
SMILES
TODAY

LET'S DO
WHAT WE
LOVE
DO A LOT
&
OF IT

YOU WILL
NEVER
BE READY
JUST
START

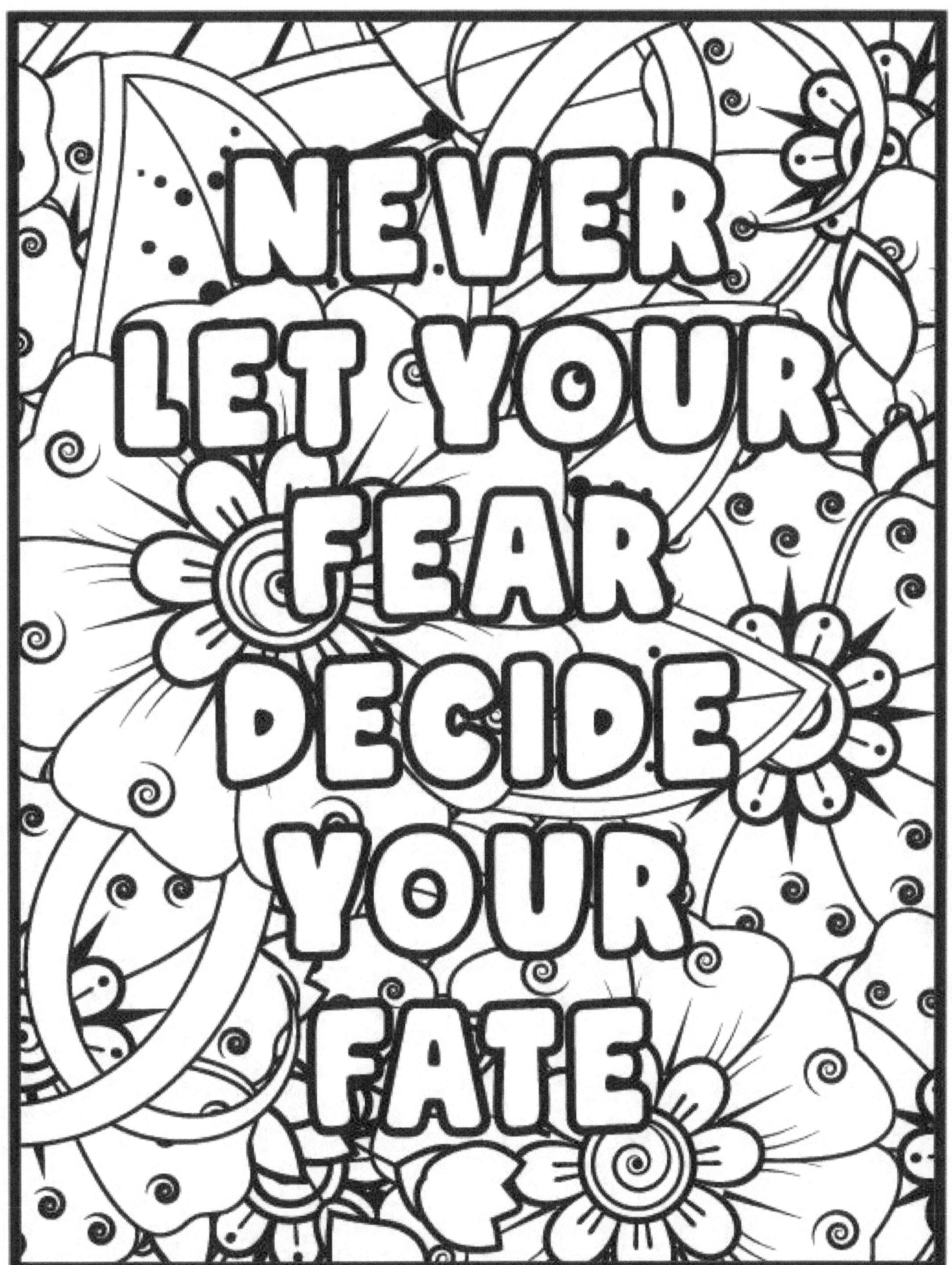

NEVER
LET YOUR
FEAR
DECIDE
YOUR
FATE

YOUR
ONLY
LIMIT
IS
YOU

WE RISE
BY
LIFTING
OTHERS

TRUST
THE
TIMING
OF
YOUR
LIFE

DON'T
WISH FOR
IT
WORK FOR
IT

NEVER
BE
AFRAID
OF
CHANGE

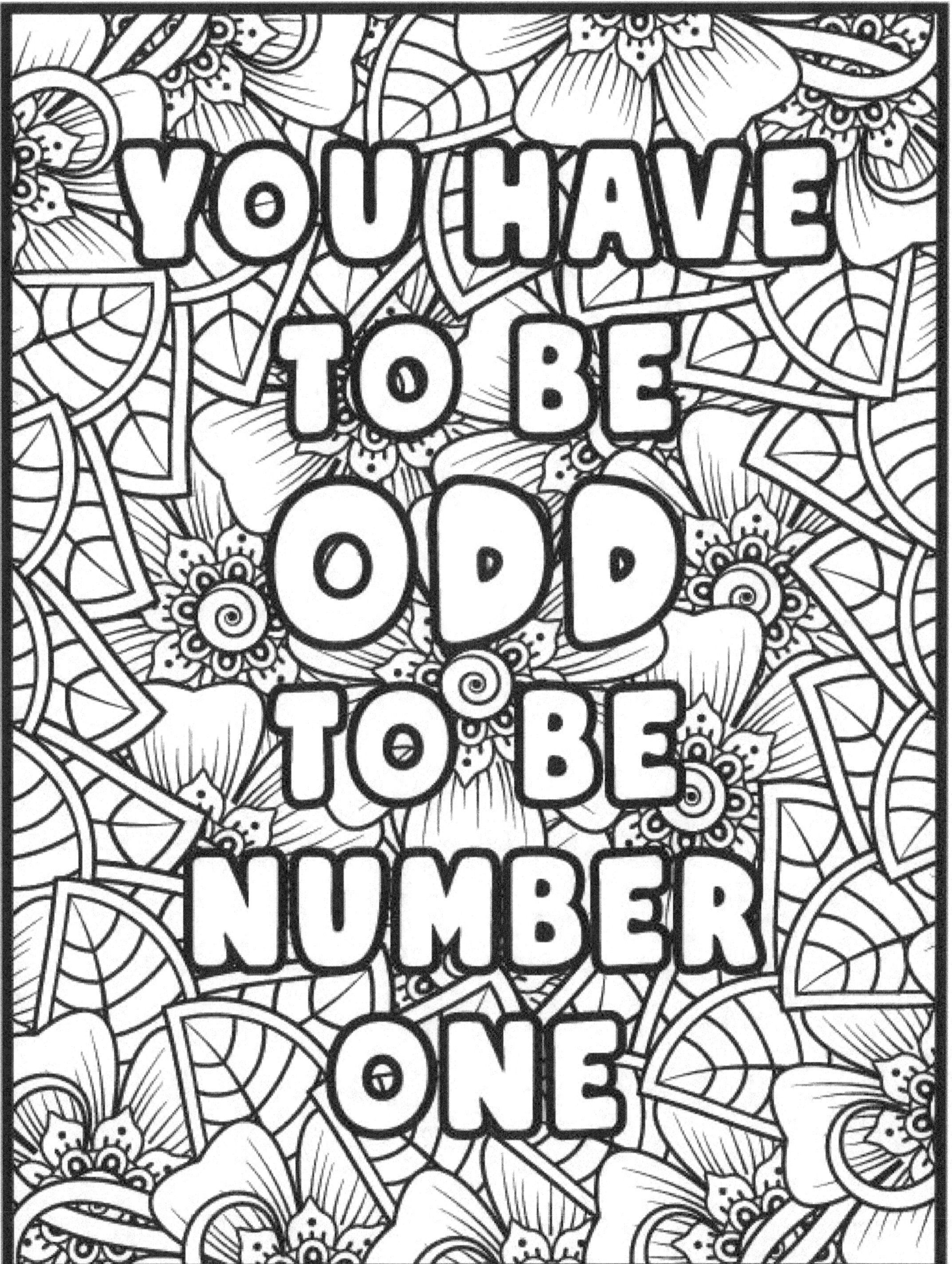

YOU HAVE
TO BE
ODD
TO BE
NUMBER
ONE

YOU ARE
BORN TO
BE REAL
NOT TO
BE
PERFECT

BELIEVE
IN
YOURSELF

TAKE A
MOMENT TO
APPRECIATE
HOW
AWESOME
YOU ARE

YOUR
ONLY
LIMIT
IS
YOU

BE THE
BEST
VERSION
OF
YOU

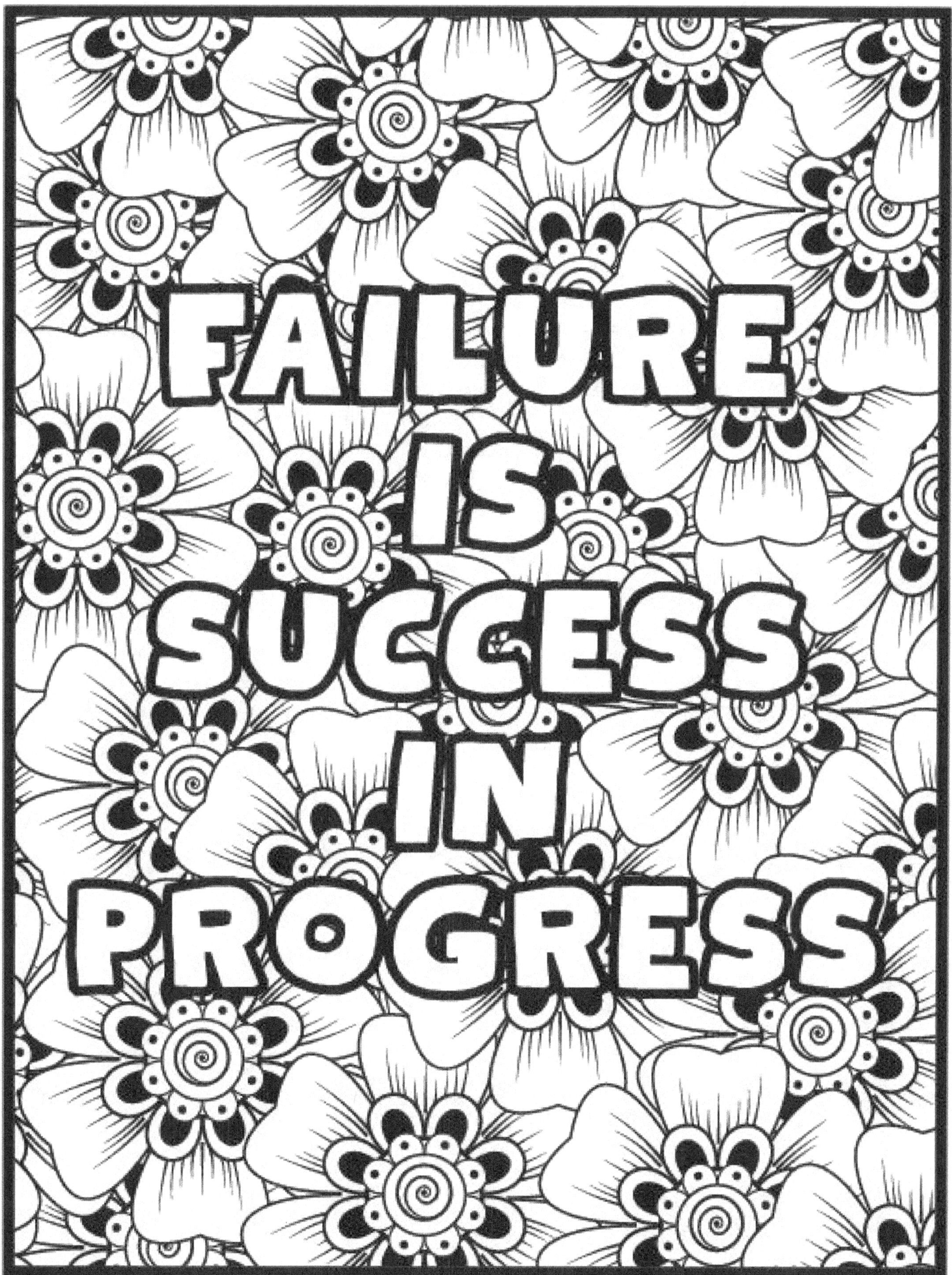

FAILURE
IS
SUCCESS
IN
PROGRESS

DON'T
STOP
UNTIL
YOU'RE
PROUD

NOTHING WILL WORK UNLESS YOU DO

YOU
CAN
DO
IT

EVERYTHING
YOU DO
NOW
IS
FOR
YOUR
FUTURE

TRY TO
BE A
RAINBOW
IN
SOMEONE'S
CLOUD

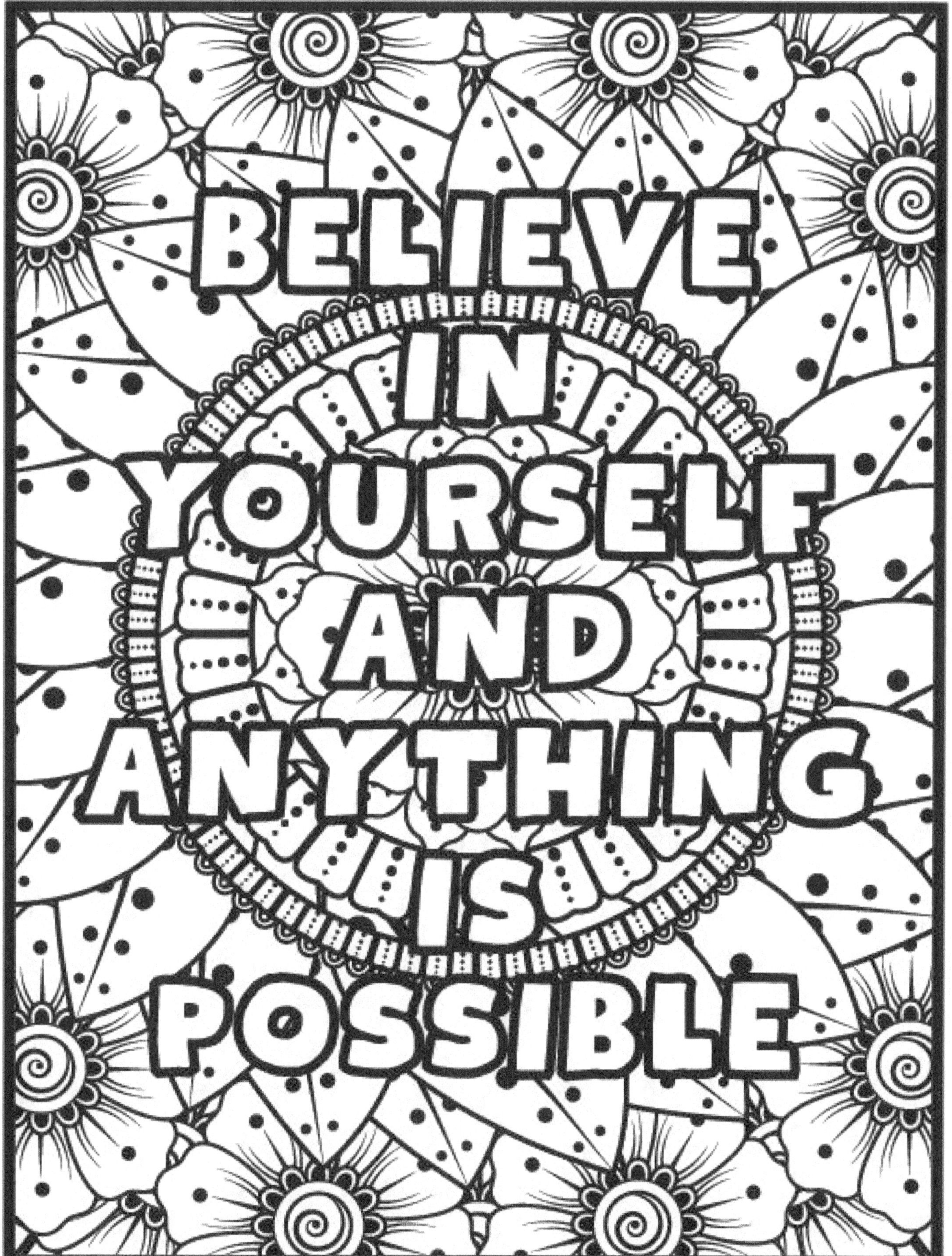

BELIEVE
IN
YOURSELF
AND
ANYTHING
IS
POSSIBLE

IT
DOESN'T
GET EASIER
YOU
JUST GET
STRONGER

IT'S A
SLOW
PROCESS
BUT
QUITTING
WON'T
SPEED
IT UP

YOU
KNOW
MY
NAME
NOT MY
STORY

BE A
WARRIOR
NOT
A
WORRIER

JUST
SAY
YIKES
AND
MOVE
ON

THE
WORST
ENEMY TO
CREATIVITY
IS
SELF-DOUBT